NORTH EASTERN STEAM

Maurice Johnson

First published 1989

ISBN 0 7110 1869 3

© Ian Allan Ltd 1989

Published by

IAN ALLAN LTD

Terminal House Shepperton TW17 8AS
Telephone: Walton-on-Thames (0932) 228950
Fax: 0932 232366   Telex: 929806 IALLAN G
Registered Office: Terminal House Shepperton TW17 8AS
Printed by Ian Allan Printing Ltd at its works at Coombelands in Runnymede,
England

Front cover: This photograph shows the end of yet another country
railway service. The line was from Morpeth to Reedsmouth Junction
via Kielder to Riccarton Junction on the Waverley route. The train is a
once-a-week pick-up goods to Woodburn and has just arrived at
Woodburn station, and is ready to shunt the yard, on 22 September
1966. *Leica IIIG 2.8 Summitar CT18 1/250, f5.6*

Back cover: Night time on Newcastle Central station. The
much-modified front-end appearance of double chimney and German
smoke deflectors of an 'A3' could send the spotters and enthusiasts
into raptures and also send them rushing about to get 'on the plate' or
take photographs by the dozen. No 60092 stands at the head of the
Manchester-Newcastle on a Friday evening, No 9 platform.
Leica IIIG 15sec, f4 PF5 fill-in flash

Right: 'V2' No 60939 is put to work on the climb towards
Chester-le-Street and Durham, and is seen just clear of Birtley station
with the 12.30 ex Newcastle — the up 'Northumbrian' — in 1961.
Agfa Silette 2.8 Agfa CT18 1/250, f5.6

Introduction

This volume on steam operation in the North Eastern Region covers a period from 1961 to the complete demise of steam traction in September 1967. The cameras used were an Agfa Silette Compur 1/500 f2.8 and a Leica IIIG with 50mm f2 Summitar and 135mm f3.5 Hector telephoto lens. Fortunately both of these cameras gave superb results of sharpness and colour. My belief that one should always try to get the foreground in focus, meant that depth of field had to be worked out with great care. This was a fine idea in good bright weather, but always a trouble when it was dull or indoors. In the early 1960s film speeds were very slow by today's standards and using 50 ASA film, pictures' could still be quite grainy and exposures had to be just right.

My close interest in railways started around 1947, when a friend and I used to watch and collect numbers, sitting on the steps of North Shore signalbox, Stockton-on-Tees. As I lived only 150yd away from the lineside I was very much aware of railway activities, with the extensive shunting yards next to North Shore box which were very busy most of the day and night. It was quite normal for me to go to bed to the sounds of the yards and hard working shunters, listening to the 'staggering' chatter of a three-cylinder Wilson Worsdell 'T1' 2-8-0 erupting into life for short bursts, and wanting to get up again to watch the sparks fly. As a result of living so close to the locomotive shed I spent a lot of time in and around steam engines and so it is no wonder that my life and business are concerned with the preservation of steam locomotives. I still remember well 40 years on the situation leading up to my first drive of a steam locomotive. I was sitting with my mate on the turntable bufferstops at Stockton shed, feeling quite warm in the sunshine and having a chew on something tasty, chatting and taking in the activity around us, when an old boy of a driver walks up — him being my mate's grandfather — and says 'You're not sitting down doing nothing again, are you?' and in his next breath says 'Come on, I've got an engine to put away'. We did not need a second telling and dashed off after him. A couple of minutes later we were climbing on to the footplate of a 'WD' 2-8-0. 'Right, youngen! Pull that regulator and let's have her up the yard and on to the ash pit.' This introduction to what the life in steam really meant, eventually had to lead to a much greater and closer interest of steam and railway activities.

This book represents a cross-section of some of the railway activities in the final years of steam operation from my library of slides. To reduce a collection of hundreds of photographs down to 60 or so was a difficult task, but hopefully it will release another small piece of history of the railways, and men of steam.

In conclusion I would like to thank Brian Cooke and Ken Harris who thought it a good idea that my photographic efforts should go public, and so give pleasure to those of us who cannot forget the passing of an era.

MAURICE JOHNSON
Grosmont
February 1989

Unless credited otherwise, all photographs are by the author.

Left: A frosty day in 1962 and steam still mostly rules. Three 'A4s', two of which were Nos 60002/60033, all have full steam and are ready to go off shed. This scene at Gateshead was typical any day right up to the end. *Leica IIIG f2 Summitar Agfa CT18*

Right: Evening sunshine and long shadows always make for good pictures. The sight and sound of this 'No 9' was nothing short of dramatic. No 92099 is just clear of South Pelaw Junction and approaching West Pelton with a heavy ore train to Consett steelworks. *Leica IIIG f2 Summitar CT18 1/250, f4*

Above: This was one of my favourite places on the Darlington-Newcastle section. It is Plawsworth Viaduct and cuttings. Well away from major roads and industry, in between trains it was so peaceful and quiet, and the complete opposite as a train went through this confined space. No 60112 *St Simon* with a down Colchester-Newcastle arrives fast and shuts off on the down gradient to Chester-le-Street. *Leica IIIG f2 Summitar CT18 1/1000, f4*

Left: A 34A King's Cross engine, takes over the 1E14 Glasgow-King's Cross train some time in 1962 and departs in fine style from Newcastle, No 10 platform. No 60015 was pulling a heavy train and had just slipped badly which accounted for the mass of black clag.
Agfa Silette Old CT18 1/125, f4

Above: Fast freight traffic was usually diagrammed to a 'V2' or 'B1', but not often a Pacific. There was always a steady stream of such traffic and most went through the back roads. Some nights at Newcastle got so busy that trains were routed through the platforms. No 60084 on this seed potato train had stopped for water in Platform 8 on its way to Scotland via Carlisle.

Leica IIIG Perutz 15sec, f4 PF5 fill-in flash

Above: A most memorable evening on the last day of 1965. A return working, York-Newcastle-York, was operated by the last working 'A1' Pacific No 60145 *St Mungo*. Just about everyone interested in steam must have been on that train. This shot shows the 'A1' standing in York after a very high-speed run from Darlington.
Leica IIIG f2 Summitar 5sec, f2 PF5 fill-in flash

7

Above: Here on a more open section of Platform 10, No 61019 *Nilghai* is working as west end pilot, and has buffered up to the stock for 1N67, the Fridays Only Manchester-Newcastle train. For some reason the train had stopped short and the wider area of platform made possible this almost broadside shot. The film on this occasion was Perutz which had a tendency to produce a lot of yellow if over exposed. In this case it helps to lighten a dark area. *Agfa Silette 2.8 Compur 15sec, f4*

Below: 'A4' No 60004, *William Whitelaw* takes water with a RCTS special in September 1965 at Stockton station standing just clear of the single span overall roof which was so typical of North Eastern traditions. Sadly in recent years the roof has been demolished and although the station is still in daily use it now appears quite abandoned.
Leica IIIG CT18 4sec, f5.6

Below: Steam on and accelerating downhill, No 60885 approaches Plawsworth at about 70mph in 1962. Usually at this point engines had been shut off and were drifting and the train was a little late, so I suspect the driver had decided to push on a bit. *Leica IIIG f2 Summitar Agfa CT18 1/1000, f4*

Below: 'A1' No 60150 *Willbrook* arrives at Darlington Bank Top with a 2.35pm Newcastle-York stopper in 1962. No whistling, rumbling roar as today, but just a quiet shuffling and the grind of brakes, then almost silence except for station sounds, doors, etc.
Leica IIIG f2 Summitar Agfa CT18 1/125, f8

Far left: In those last years of nearly full steam workings, with just a hint of the Type 4 or a 'Deltic', I used to buy a cheap day return from Newcastle to York, Carlisle or maybe Berwick. On this occasion in 1962, I went to York and had just got off the 2.35pm ex-Newcastle at Darlington — steam, of course. The next thing someone shouted 'V2' and No 60916 went past in cracking form with a northbound fitted mixed.
Leica IIIG f2 Summitar Agfa CT18 1/250, f4

Left: 'A4' No 60004 digs in its heels and restarts a heavy special away from Plawsworth station (Gateshead) and takes the Leamside line to the south, 19 September 1965. This was the original old northeast line and bypassed the city of Durham and connected with the main line at Ferryhill.
Leica IIIG f2 Summitar Agfa CT18 1/500, f11

Far left: On a Friday evening in 1962 No 60143 *Sir Walter Scott* buffers up to the empty stock of the old 'Tees-Tyne Pullman' on Platform 8 at Newcastle Central and gets his fire ready before leaving with the stock to Heaton carriage sidings.
Leica IIIG 10sec, f4

Left: A nice shiny 'A3' and a very wet train head south from Scotland having just taken water to excess on Luker troughs south of Belford, Northumberland. This was some place to be! Just sitting, watching and chewing a 'sarnie'. The train is a special, some time in August 1964.
Leica IIIG 135mm Hector

Above: One Saturday in 1966 while watching out for a coke train from Norwood, I was very surprised to hear the high-speed beat of a Gresley '3' coming from behind. Main line steam turns were very much in decline and this was something of a bonus. 'V2' No 60836, which was later cut up in Dunston, was approaching Newcastle very fast through Low Fell with a heavy parcels, having taken over from a failed Type 4 at Darlington.
Leica IIIG 135mm Hector 1/250, f4.5

Right: This 'A3' driver must have thought he might be late for his tea as he blasted the locomotive away with what must have been full regulator and most of the gear, and I would think, most of the fireman's hard work with it. The locomotive heads out of Platform 8 with a Saturday Berwick stopper in 1962. *Agfa Silette 2.8 Agfa CT18 1/250, f4*

BRITISH RAILWAYS
ELECTRIFIED LINES

DANGER

IT IS FATAL TO TOUCH
THE ELEVATED RAILS

Right: 'V2' No 60868 working hard on the climb from Chester-le-Street to Durham, is on the up Red Bank parcels and is crossing Plawsworth Viaduct. In the latter years this turn also served for crew training.
Leica IIIG 135mm Hector
Agfa CT18 1/250, f3.5

Far right: This shot shows a typical nightly scene which one could see when visiting Newcastle Central. The stock of the Royal Mail travelling post office is standing in the centre roads prior to use and is being steam-heated by the use of pilot engine 'V3' No 67620, a former 64B Haymarket locomotive in September 1963.
Leica IIIG Agfa CT18 1/8, f5.6

Above: In the extremely cold, freezing conditions of 1963 there were a lot of diesel failures due to frost, and steam was again supreme. Here station pilot engine 'V3' No 67653 stands with a full head of steam in the back roads of Platform 10 Newcastle Central, on Friday 4 January 1963.

20   *Leica IIIG f2 Summitar Agfa CT18 20sec, f4*

Right: 'J72' No 69025, one of a batch built by BR from 1949 to a Wilson Worsdell design of 1898, is seen at the type of duty for which it was designed — shunting a fitted van train on Platform 8, at the west end of Newcastle Central.

Leica IIIG f2 Summitar Agfa CT18 7sec, f4

Left: Inside the beautiful old North Eastern train shed of Alnwick station. 'K1' No 62050 stands ready with the return shuttle to Alnmouth, 23 April 1966. *Leica IIIG 1/8, f4*

Above: Another evening on the Northumberland coast sees No 62050 arrive at Alnmouth on the 6.55pm pick-up goods and passenger from Alnwick. *Leica IIIG   Agfa CT18 1/125, f4*

Below: In the summer evenings a trip out to Carlisle or Berwick was always pleasant, and if it included calling in at a junction station like Morpeth or Alnmouth to see what there was in the way of steam, the evening would be complete. Alnmouth station was in a beautiful setting on the hillside looking out over the village and the North Sea. No 62021 takes water before going on shed on 23 May 1966. *Leica IIIG CT18 1/125, f4*

Right: In the last years of North Eastern steam, ex-LMS engines were pushed into our area. Class 4MTs ('Flying Pigs') were in regular use, and on this occasion even got in on the last Woodburn pick-up. No 43063 departs from Woodburn for Morpeth on 29 September 1966. *Leica IIIG CT18 1/250, f5.6*

Left: New Hartley, just south of Blyth, Northumberland, was originally a junction station down to Monkseaton and Whitley Bay. The coast branch was closed in the early 1960s by the 'Beeching Axe'. On 29 April 1966 'J27' No 65857 works a heavy coal train towards Seaton Delaval. The old station gas lights still existed from times gone by.
Leica IIIG 1/500, f4

Above: 'K1' No 62048, its fireman working hard on the heavy gradient from Cemetery North Junction, Hartlepool, passes Monk Hesleden in 1964. At this point on the line the track was split by an embankment. This had been the base of an old wagonway complete with square blocks.
Leica IIIG Agfa CT18 1/250, f4

Above: One of the few named engines of the 'V2' class, No 60809 was one of only seven out of 184 engines that were named. *The Snapper, The East Yorkshire Regiment, The Duke of York's Own* — always a delight to see for spotters of all ages, is approaching Durham Viaduct with a down fitted freight from York early in 1962.
Agfa Silette Agfa CT18 1/500, f4

Right: A profile of speed: 'V2' No 60867 is in full cry on the up main passing Low Fell in 1962. After a signal check it had to get a move on to clear the section for a following express.
Agfa Silette CT18 1/125, f11 pan shot

Above: A southbound coal train climbs up into Bedlington past the junction to Hepscott and Morpeth in June 1966. In the once very busy Northumberland coalfields, mineral traffic was heavy and track repair gangs would be found hard pushed to jack and repack the permanent way between trains. No 65880 eases a train from Ashington over a section which had just been repaired a few minutes before.

Leica IIIG   Agfa CT18   1/250, f5.6

Above: Riddles Ministry of Supply 'Austerity' locomotives purchased by British Railways in 1948 were introduced in 1943. The 'WD' '8F' 2-8-0 had a tractive effort of 34,215lb and was capable of hauling very heavy loads just about anywhere. A long train of coal empties hauled by No 90479 approaches Billingham-on-Tees from Norton, sometime in 1964.
Leica IIIG Agfa CT18 1/250, f4

Above: Whenever possible a visit to Newcastle Central station would nearly always be rewarding, as on this occasion just after lunch on a Saturday, 'V3' No 67646 was being coupled up for empty stock working to Heaton carriage sidings sometime in 1961. *Agfa Silette 2.8 Agfa CT18 1/60, f8*

Right: This was an unusual place for a Class 9 locomotive to be. Much over-powered for the duty, No 92099 is standing in the goods roads of Alnwick station, having worked much of the day on the shuttle to the junction station of Alnmouth. This was the last day of steam operation on the branch. *Leica IIIG Agfa CT18 1/125, f8*

Right: Alnmouth, near Alnwick in Northumberland, was a market town junction station complete with MPD and sidings. In years gone by Alnwick had been linked with a country line to Wooler and Coldstream. On the last day of steam operation — 18 June 1966 — the motive power was, of all things, a '9F'. Well turned out it was, but completely over-powered for two coaches. No 92099 is waiting on the down main ready to leave for Alnwick.
D. C. Johnson Regulete Pronto 1/250, f8

Far right: The nearest section of railway from home was down in the Team Valley at Low Fell station. Here could be seen high-speed arrivals, hard-worked departures, and on the slow lines numerous goods workings of all types. A 'Q6' (North Eastern Class T2) 0-8-0 goods locomotive seen topping the steep climb of Low Fell yard bank with oil tanks for Consett on 27 April 1966.
Leica IIIG 1/250, f5.6

Above: As the winter period set in, certain locomotives had to be readied for all-weather operations to ensure that the mineral traffic kept moving. The fitting of an offset snowplough made it possible for a locomotive such as a 'Q6' to push its way through bad snow conditions and fulfil its duties. This picture shows No 63395 working hard and clean on the bank near Seaton station, with empties for South Hetton.

D. C. Johnson Regulete Pronto 1/250, f8

Above: An unknown 'WD' gets to grips with Ryhope Bank with coal empties from Sunderland to Easington in 1966. The strong westerly wind helped to clear the smoke and steam from the engine. It also blew the sound away until the last 100yd.
Leica IIIG   Agfa CT18   1/250, f4

Above: A local country pick-up freight accelerating hard for the climb into the Northumberland hills near Cambo just west of the junction station of Scotsgap. No 65842 was in good fettle and the fireman put on a good show to order.
Leica IIIG f2 Summitar CT18 1/250, f4

Right: 'J27' No 65842 stands at Scotsgap with coal and goods for the Woodburn and Bellingham area of Northumberland.
Leica IIIG Agfa CT18 1/60, f5.6

Below: 'J27' No 65894 here seen amid its normal duties around the Sunderland industrial area at Pallion station and is setting back into E. Jopling's foundry on the last steam operated pick-up goods on 29 August 1967.
D. C. Johnson Regulete Pronto 1/125, f8

Right: One of the most powerful eight-coupled locomotives built which survived in full service into the early 1960s. The 'Q7', introduced in 1919 for the North Eastern Railway, was designed by Raven. With a tractive effort of 36,965lb it was still a very good match for the modern '9F'. No 63460 is seen being serviced on Darlington MPD. The engine still exists and resides on the NYMR at Grosmont.
Leica IIIG f2 Summitar Agfa CT18 1/125, f8

Above: The line to Consett steelworks was twisty and steep. It always commanded a good engine and crew and if things did not quite work out, engines would quite often stop at Beamish for a blow-up. In this case No 92060 was well on top of the job even on the reverse curves just above Stanley, with diesel assistance. *Leica IIIG 135mm Hector 1/250, f5.6*

Right: No 65869 with the regulator in the top of the cab turns away from the coast line at Ryhope and begins the gradient of Seaton Bank with a rake of empties for South Hetton. *Leica IIIG 1/250, f4*

Below: Darlington was a busy industrial area and the railway serviced most of it, consequently a lot of freight arrived and departed most of the day. This was shunted and moved about by various small locomotives and ex-WD 'J94s' were in regular use. No 68043 is seen passing on the through line with an inter-yard shuttle of vans and steel flats, winter 1962. *Leica IIIG Agfa CT18 1/250, f4*

Right: Here we have steam and steel together. No 65872 shunts in Austin & Pickersgill's shipyard after arriving with the Southwick pick-up, running light engine to collect its van under the overhead gantry cranes on 2 March 1966. In the days of steam, coal, steel and ships were very much part of Sunderland and the River Wear. *D. C. Johnson*

Left: Inside what was known as the Pacific shed at Gateshead. The sunshine through the windows did a lot to improve what would have been a very gloomy place. Here on the centre road 'Green Arrow' class No 60964 stands prominent with representatives of three other Gresley classes around it.
Leica IIIG Agfa CT18 1/15, f5.6

Above: If ever an example of an engine type should have been preserved it would have been a 'V3' 2-6-2T 4MT, introduced in 1939, developed from Gresley's 'V1' of 1930. With its three cylinders, and 86 tons, it could lift most loads without trouble. No 67691 (52B) has just arrived at Platform 10, Newcastle Central with an evening Newbiggin parcels pick-up.
Leica IIIG f2 Summitar 10sec, f4

Above: The soft sunshine falling across the shed yard caught this Pacific just right, as the fireman made his final preparations to go off shed. No 60151 is standing outside the Pacific shed at Gateshead MPD.
Leica IIIG f2 Summitar Agfa CT18 1/250, f4

Right: There is always a different feeling and character change when a railway station is visited at night time. In the days of steam the sights and sounds were almost magnetic, and anyone with steam in their blood will, no doubt, have spent many a cold, cold night out, where one positively glowed as night trains came and went about their duties. No 60051 has just arrived on Platform 10 with the Manchester-Newcastle 1N67 on Friday 15 February 1963.
Leica IIIG f2 Summitar 5sec, f5.6

Left: A quiet scene. Tweedmouth was one of those havens of peace. There was no heavy industry and very little pollution, except possibly when the charge cleaner had an extra one or two to light up. 'V2' No 60836 is being turned ready for a return trip to Edinburgh. *Leica IIIG Agfa CT18 1/60, f5.6*

Above: A Saturday visit to Darlington locomotive works would always be rewarding. Many a new engine or rebuild had been completed within the works or its erecting shop. Seen here are two of Gresley's best classes — an 'A4' without cladding and an 'A3'. No 60052 became one of the last two

'A3s' running and saw service on many a last fling special. *Leica IIIG Agfa CT18 1/30, f4*

Far left: No 92060 arrives at Beamish station on 1 May 1966 with a full load of ore for Consett steelworks. By the amount of black smoke both of the crew must have been shovelling and they still had to stop for a blow-up.
Leica IIIG   Agfa CT18   1/250, f8

Left: A lovely evening and long shadows show this setting very well. 'J27' No 65882 is finished for this shift as it stops at Silksworth signalbox to hand back the single line token on 31 August 1967.
Leica IIIG   Agfa CT18   1/125, f8

53

Left: Two trains are seen here travelling in opposite directions both with freshly loaded coal on 13 September 1966. This traffic movement was common to see at Bedlington station as it was — and still is — the junction from Morpeth and Blyth.

Leica IIIG f2 Summitar Agfa CT18 1/250, f4

Above: The last operating turn on the West Woodburn branch was operated by a very well-cleaned 4MT No 43063. The train is seen departing from Knowesgate across the A696 on 29 September 1966. *Leica IIIG CT18 1/250, f5.6*

Above: A 'Jubilee' 5XP on a North Eastern goods shed at one time must have been unthinkable. As steam traction declined around the country, the dreaded railtour managed to creep into all sorts of corners. Blyth North, Northumberland, with its North Sea view seemed a most incongruous location for No 45562 *Alberta* but this shot from the coal stage ramp on 10 June 1967 made a fine picture anyway.

Right: On the line that once linked the East Coast main line from Northallerton on the Midland at Garsdale (Hawes Junction). The line is now the northeast's longest freight branch and is still operating to quarries at Redmire. This picture taken by the summit board between Redmire and Leyburn shows No 62005, now preserved on the NYMR, assisted by a Type 2 diesel with an SLS special on 20 May 1967. The 'K1' was withdrawn a few weeks later.

Leica IIIG   Agfa CT18   1/125, f11

Leica IIIG   Agfa CT18   1/125, f11

Left: An afternoon to remember, but not completely, as notes and timings seem to have disappeared for this working. It would be a Saturday afternoon in 1962, myself and a mate had met up, probably for a trip on the 2.35pm Newcastle-York stopper, usually hauled by an 'A1'. We got a surprise as this large Raven 4-6-0 arrived on Platform 9 with a passenger special which was a Durham branches railtour. No 61418 was introduced as a 'B16/3' in 1944 and was a Thompson rebuild of a 'B16/1' to Walschaerts valve gear. With a tractive effort of 30,030lb it was the largest North Eastern 4-6-0.
Agfa Silette Early Agfa CT18 1/60, f4

Left: Whilst waiting to photograph a Newcastle-York stopper just south of Darlington Bank Top station in 1964, the south yard shunter came to a stand nearby and almost immediately a 'K1', No 62048, came round from the Stockton line with a weedkiller train in full operation. Consequently both No 68010 and myself got a good extra wash.
Leica IIIG 1/250, f4

Right: On a clear, windy day, a telephoto lens is used to capture No 63459 working easily, being pushed by a Type 3 diesel past West Pelton on the heavy grade to Beamish and Consett. Durham provides the backdrop, with the Penshaw Monument in the far background.
Leica IIIG 135mm Hector Agfa CT18 1/250, f4.5

Above: Wilson Worsdell introduced his larger boiler 'J27' (or 'P3') in 1906 which was developed from his 'J26' for larger steam capacity on long slogging work. On this occasion speed was of the essence when the lads wanted to get finished.

No 65879 is seen running fast downhill into Sunderland past Ryhope with coal from South Hetton. At sea in the background is a gas test drilling rig.

Leica IIIG 135mm Hector Agfa CT18 1/250, f4.5

Above: The steel trestle bridge over the River Wansbeck near Ashington is the centrepiece of this shot. A 'J27' with a short coal train for Blyth heads south high above the river.
Leica IIIG   Agfa CT18   1/250, f4

61

Above: 'J72' No 68723 is seen one Saturday in 1962 in North Eastern green; this engine was one of the first batch built from 1898 and ended its days shunting the various goods sheds and sidings around Newcastle with over 60 operational years of service. *Agfa Silette 1/500, f4*

Below: Here it is a little obvious that the enthusiast had been doing a spot of cleaning, as compressor-fitted '9F' No 92063 stood on the ore drops at Consett steelworks on 19 November 1966. This was the last steam-operated ore train to Consett and it was quite obvious on the trip up to Consett that the engine and crew were right on top of the job, as a considerable amount of time was knocked off the schedule, and in quite a few places couplings had been kept tight between the wagons and the Type 4 banker.

Leica IIIG   50mm Summitar   U/V filter   CT18   1/125, f4

Above: Inside Sunderland roundhouse on 8 September 1967, the last night of operational steam in very much the heartland of what had been the North Eastern Railway. To see all these very clean engines together was nice, but also very sad, for in normal service engines were usually *only* clean when ex-works.

Leica IIIG f2 Summitar 2min, f4